LAID OFF, BUT *Not* LAID OUT

Copyright © 2010 by Kimberly C. Kisner

All rights reserved. No part of this publication may be reproduced, stored in a retrieval system or transmitted in any form or by any means electronic, mechanical, photocopying, recording or otherwise, except by a reviewer who may quote brief passages for review purposes, without the prior written permission of the author.

Published by
OPOL Publishing
Dayton, OH

For more information, please contact Author at
laidoffnotlaidout@yahoo.com

Cover design by Cathi Stevenson / Book Cover Express

1st Printing, 2010

Printed and bound in the United States of America

ALL RIGHTS RESERVED

TESTIMONIALS

"*Laid Off, but Not Laid Out* is an excellent read. I've been through several layoffs myself, so I understand what Kimberly went through. I think this book provides real-life solutions to real life situations, and I think readers will appreciate that."

— Charlotte LaTonya Mayo

"*Laid Off, but Not Laid Out* bears it all. Kimberly's narrative is engaging and her timeless nuggets of wisdom are on time. She provides great insights that might escape your mind if you are ever faced with the unpleasant experience of being laid off. And even if you never go through a layoff, this book is still a must read! Kimberly gives solid advice that will help you get ahead and stay ahead professionally."

— Keenan Walker

LAID OFF, BUT *Not* LAID OUT

TIPS FOR SURVIVING A LAYOFF

Kimberly C. Kisner

Atlanta · GA

This book is dedicated to my mother Sarah L. Kisner and father Pastor Gerald D. Kisner for without you two, I would not be here to make this book a reality. And a special dedication to my grandmother's Mattie B. Kisner and Laura E. Beck , who passed on the gift of writing to me.

ACKNOWLEDGEMENTS

I would like to give special thanks to God, for without him the vision to make this book a reality would have not been possible.

J. Thomas Maultsby of *OPOL Publishing* — Who set me on the path to self-publishing.

Eric Norton — For "Truly" believing in me. Thanks friend.

Keenan Walker — For stepping in when I needed to make this book come to life.

Tiphanie Watson of *Pulse Entertainment Group* — For helping me get the word out. Love you girl!

Cathie Stevenson — Your cover says it all! Thanks for seeing my vision.

LeVoyd Carter of *Joseph Alexander Photography* — For making me look beautiful.

Malika — Thank you for making my face a masterpiece!

Samuel E. Kisner II — Love you baby bro! Thanks for giving me inspiration.

By purchasing this book, you agree to the following: This publication is designed to provide accurate information about the subject matter covered. It is offered with the understanding that the author and publisher are not engaged in rendering medical or psychological service. This book is not intended to be a substitute for therapy or professional advice.

CONTENTS

Foreword	xiii
Introduction	1
Chapter 1: The First Layoff	5
Chapter 2: Kim has Left the Building	9
Chapter 3: Grieving the Layoff	13
Chapter 4: The Job Search	19
Chapter 5: Another Layoff?	23
Chapter 6: More Than Just a Mobile Network	29
Chapter 7: Stop...Wait a Minute...Self-Inflicted Layoff	33
Chapter 8: Just When I Thought It was Safe	41
Chapter 9: Oh My.....Not Again!	49
Chapter 10: Out of Two Jobs...Now What?	55
Chapter 11: I'm a Survivor...I'm Not Gonna Give Up!	59
Chapter 12: Friendship and Money	65
Chapter 13: Can't Take It Anymore!	69
Chapter 14: The Interview	73
Chapter 15: Healthcare and the Art of Negotiation	79
Chapter 16: Get Out of Your Own Way – Make IT Happen!	83
Chapter 17: Money isn't Everything	87
Chapter 18: The Layoff Tool Kit	93
Additional Resources	97

FOREWORD

There is a saying that goes, twenty percent of life is about what happens to you but eighty percent of life is about how we respond to it. It is tragic that many of us allow what has happened to us to define us. We enthrone our negative experiences and give them so much power that they begin to dictate to us and even shape us. We allow these happenings to influence our mentalities and ultimately, shape our realities.

The awesome thing about Kimberly Kisner's book, **Laid Off, but Not Laid Out**, is it helps us to understand that we do not have to allow our history to determine our destiny. The very title of this book by Kimberly Kisner, who has personally had her share of layoffs, reminds us that being downsized does not mean being down and out or even being, sized down.

So often, people who lose positions with companies begin to feel inadequate. Kimberly Kisner's book helps us to remember that although we may lose a position at work, we still have a position in God and Jesus Christ. Whereas a job can be temporary, our position in the Lord and His Kingdom is eternal. No matter what has happened to us, we are who God says we are and can achieve what God promises concerning our lives.

In other words, our place is one of victory in spite of loss. **Laid Off, but Not Laid Out** not only shares this message, but gives us awesome practical strategies for living victoriously in the face of what can be one of life's most trying circumstances.

– Pastor DeQuincy M. Hentz
Shiloh Baptist Church – New Rochelle, NY

INTRODUCTION

MY NAME IS KIMBERLY KISNER and I am a thirty-something intelligent, educated, well-experienced young woman. And for the most part of my life since graduating from undergrad, I've had a pretty good career.

I've worked at some of the top companies. I have been fortunate to have pretty much worked in my field of study ever since graduation – and yes that is big, because many people go to school for one thing and end up being in a profession that has nothing to do with what they received their degree in.

Now, I've had my share of career ups and downs, but I honestly thought that I would be in a stable job for a little while, unless I was the one who made the job change. In fact, my goal was to work in my last position, save money and then start my own marketing company, Perceptions Marketing Group (Shameless plug).

Well, obviously the Man upstairs had another plan for me. So when I went to work that morning and discovered that I was being laid off after only being there a year, I was shocked. I honestly couldn't believe that this was happening. In fact, when I told my friends and my family what happened, I was cracking up when I said to them, "You know, I

Kimberly C. Kisner

should write a book about being laid off and how to survive it. I mean I've been laid off so many times in my life, I feel like I'm an expert."

Well, what started out as a joke, turned into a reality.

I was taking a shower one morning, just thinking out loud while making fun of my personal career crisis and I started talking to God. Then something came over me…something got within my spirit and all of sudden it was like a big spot light shining on me. "Yes, I shall write a book about being laid off."

Then one night when I was sleeping, the title of the book came to me. "Laid off but not Laid Out!" I knew right then and there that this was the book that I was supposed to write, a book that I had to write. I knew this book had less to do with making money, than it had to do with utilizing my talents/gifts as well as my experiences to help others.

And thus; you are reading a little book called "Laid off, but not Laid Out." I wrote this book for you.

If you bought this book then you must have realized that you can benefit from it. I'm not going to lie to you, this book is not going to give you all the answers about how to land a job or how to avoid being laid off, but what it will do is provide you with real-life guidance from a personal perspective. I'm not going to tell you that now you are laid off, go and follow your dreams. That was not my experience. I'm just "keeping it real," as they say."

However, what this book will do is help you to survive and offer suggestions for how to make it during your layoff experience. If you do have some dreams or goals, then by all means go for it. But let's be realistic, when you lose your job the first thing that you are thinking about is not necessarily pursing your life long dream of becoming an actor, producer or a business owner. Your main concern is, "How am I going to make it and still pay my bills?" This book will give you guidelines and suggestions based on my personal experiences. At a minimum, I hope you take comfort in knowing that you are not the only one going through this and you too can come out on top. You just have to stay prayerful, positive and motivated. Having a support system also helps.

I hope you enjoy this book and I would love to hear your feedback after you've read it. Please send me your comments to **laidoffnotlaidout@yahoo.com**.

Kimberly C. Kisner

CHAPTER 1
THE FIRST LAY-OFF

IT WAS 6:00 A.M. as my alarm went off loudly. I reluctantly turned over to shut it off. I got up out of bed and engaged in my usual routine of getting ready for a long day of work. As I'm driving to work happy about my decision to move back to Atlanta, Ga. I thanked God that I was able to land a job in such a short amount of time.

Granted, the job that I was on my way to was not the dream job, but it got me back to my old stomping ground. I head to work in the Cobb Galleria area , I park my car and high oh , high oh, it's off to work I go. I got on the elevator and make my way up to the top floor where my office was. I didn't have a lot on my plate this particular day so I just checked my e-mail and proceeded to complete some administrative duties. Before I knew it, it was time for me to grab some lunch.

I left for lunch as usual and enjoyed the hour vacation from my job. After lunch, I came back to the office and was told by my boss that he wanted to see me in the conference room. To my surprise, I had no idea what this was about, considering that I had only been on this particular job for one month. So, I went to the conference room where I was greeted by not only my boss, but also by a Human Resources representative,

(HR). Then the unthinkable happened. The HR representative informed me that the company was being bought out, and therefore, needed to lay off some people and I was one of them.

At that moment, I couldn't hear anything the woman was saying nor my boss. In fact, I suddenly became mute. It was like I was having an out of body experience, "Is this really happening to me?" And the kicker was since I had only been in that position for one month, I was only entitled to receive 2 weeks severance. "What???!! First of all, what is severance," (This is what I said to myself).

I immediately began to cry. It was as though someone told me that I was going to jail. Once I heard what I thought was the end of my career, I was told I had to leave the premises immediately and that I had to be escorted by security. (Side Note: what did they think I was going to do? Steal a stapler, or perhaps some ballpoint pens? Escort me? Now that was too funny. I mean is this prom?) So I did as I was commanded to do, and I left the building. I got into my car and then broke down in hysterics. I didn't know what to do next. I had rent to pay and other bills and now I have no job and let us not forget that I just moved back to Atlanta not too long ago. Now, what am I supposed to do?

For those of you who are not familiar with this scenario, the series of events that I just described is what may occur when you go through a LAYOFF. By definition a layoff is the "elimination of jobs, often without regard to employee performance, usually when a company is experiencing financial difficulties." Those of you who are familiar with a layoff, can most likely relate to the experience that I just described.

Being a victim of a layoff is not something that I wish on anyone. It can be one of the most difficult and lowest points of your life - that is, if you let it. This is one of the reasons that I wrote this book. I wrote it for those of you who have no clue as to what to do when you are faced with

Kimberly C. Kisner

a layoff. I also wrote this book for those who just need some guidance and encouragement to deal with a layoff situation. I sincerely hope that the following tips and words of encouragement help to get you through your layoff period. Next is tip number one.

TIP 1
MAINTAIN YOUR COMPUSURE AND DO NOT CRY IN FRONT OF YOUR BOSS AND HR.

Ok, I know that hearing you no longer have a job, which was your bread and butter, can be a horrific experience. However, are you familiar with the term, "Never let them see you sweat?" Well, in this case, "Never let them see you cry!"

It is imperative that you remain calm, cool and collected. The best thing you can do is to have a straight face, and control your emotions. The reason I say this is because you want to make sure that you are focused on what HR and your boss are saying to you. And most important, you want to make sure you understand all of the particulars that come along with your lay-off, like what happens to your health benefits? And most especially, how much severance will you be receiving?

For those of you who are not acquainted with severance pay, it is money that an employer might want to provide to an employee who is leaving their employment. Normal circumstances that can warrant severance pay may include layoffs, job elimination, and mutual agreement to part ways for whatever reason. Severance pay usually amounts to a week or two of pay for each year of service to the company. However, at times there are exceptions to that rule. Hence, the reason you don't need to break out crying is because if you are crying, you won't be able to digest the information properly, especially if you are wiping snot from your nose with tears streaming down your face.

Kimberly C. Kisner

Another reason you need to be in a rational state-of-mind is because you want to make sure that you write down all of your accumulated vacation, as well as any personal or sick time. The reason you need to be aware of this information is because some companies do not pay severance toward all forms of paid time.

Another good idea, since you have your boss in the room and the HR rep., is to ask for a letter of recommendation. Do not push the point if you know within the depths of your soul that you really haven't been the best employee. In addition to a letter of recommendation, you may want to inquire about the continuance of your insurance benefits, any annual bonuses that may be allotted to you, perhaps the chance to do some consulting work with the company and outplacement services that may be available to you.

To Do List

1. Do not cry.
2. Do keep track of unused vacation and sick time.
3. Do ask for recommendation letter.
4. Do ask about continued health care benefits and severance pay.

CHAPTER 2

KIM HAS LEFT THE BUILDING

AFTER MY EXIT FROM THE BUILDING, I pulled myself together and headed back to my apartment, which incidentally I was sub-leasing from a friend who moved to San Francisco. I did what any normal twenty-something young woman would do, I called my mommy! Thank goodness on that particular Friday, my mom was on her way to visit me in Atlanta from Cleveland, so I knew that she was going to have sympathy for me and tell me to pack up my bags and head back home to the nest and live with her. Yes, I knew everything was going to be OK once mommy came to town. Well, contrary to what I thought was going to happen, my mother said just the opposite. She reminded me that it was my idea to move back to Hotlanta in the first place and that she was not going to allow me to give up on what I wanted to do. She said, that I was going to have to stay in Atlanta for 6 more months, and if I didn't obtain a job within that time frame, then I could move back home. What??? I really thought she was on something. I mean, how could she tell her only daughter that she had to stay in Atlanta no matter what? I mean, I didn't have a job or any money. How was I going to survive? Well, I did what my mom said because I had no other choice.

In addition to staying in Atlanta based on my mother's (and what I thought was bad) advice, it was also the first time I really had any involvement with the government of the United States. Through the government, I was introduced to a little thing called unemployment assistance. How cool I thought it was to get paid approximately a little more than $200 every week while not working. Now, keep in mind signing up for unemployment benefits is no easy feat. But I knew that this was the only form of income that I could get in a short amount of time. So, I applied for unemployment benefits. Which brings me to Tip #2:

TIP 2
APPLY FOR UNEMPLOYMENT AS SOON AS POSSIBLE.

Now, this tip is crucial for your interim situation of being unemployed. You must utilize the "free money" so-to-speak. Heck, in most cases your company has already paid for unemployment benefits. Once your severance has run out, you are entitled to receive an unemployment check every week from your states office. Keep in mind that each state varies as to the amount of money you are entitled to receive on a weekly basis. However, I suggest you don't wait until your severance runs out completely. In fact, you should go to the unemployment office immediately upon receiving your official separation letter stating that your company no longer needs your services.

Make sure to make copies of the separation letter for your files and for the local state office where you will have to register to receive your unemployment benefits.

Yes, being laid off is not very glamorous and it can be very stressful. Being laid off is also like suffering from the loss of a relative. When you have lost someone, it takes time to get over that loss and come to terms with it. So you see, experiencing the loss of a job, can be comparable to experiencing the loss of a loved one.

Kimberly C. Kisner

So in some ways it is comforting to know that you are not the only one going through this experience....Hey, as the song says, "You are not Alone." (R.I.P Michael Jackson)

To Do List

1. Do register for unemployment benefits as soon as possible.
2. Do make copies of your separation papers from the company.
3. Do call your support system (i.e. mother, father, siblings, spouse or significant other for moral and emotional support).

Kimberly C. Kisner

CHAPTER 3

GRIEVING THE LAYOFF

THINK OF BEING LAID OFF as something that you have to grieve. In dealing with grief, you are going to experience a wide range of emotions: shock, disbelief, denial, anger, depression, detachment and then finally acceptance. Being able to understand and grasp the concept of the grieving process will ultimately help you to deal with the entire traumatic experience of losing your job. The following key points will help you to get through the grieving process associated with your lay-off:

Stage 1: Shock & Disbelief

The first response to your layoff is shock and disbelief. Yes, it is difficult to accept or comprehend the reality of losing your job. In fact, you may feel a slight numbness over your entire body, followed by confusion and the inability to think straight. Along with having feelings of disbelief and shock, there will also be bouts with denial. And because you are in denial, you can't seem to function normally as you do when you are working. You may even find it difficult to want to explore other alternatives to making ends meet.

Stage 2: Anger & Extremely Emotional

As you begin to bring yourself out of the intense fog that covers your life right now, due to not having a job to go to every day, you will begin to comprehend what is actually happening to you and know that it's not a dream as articulated in the famous song by The Temptations which says – "It's just my imagination." During this stage, you will also feel very hurt as though this were a personal attack against you. You will also be frustrated and feel like you have nowhere to go or do not know what to do. Most important, you will feel anger towards your boss (who may or may not have anything to do with your layoff), the company and perhaps some of your colleagues.

Stage 3: Depression & Detachment

At this particular stage, you may experience some feelings of guilt – you know, thinking about what you could have done better as it related to your job performance. Or maybe you start thinking about if you just came in a few minutes earlier or stayed a few minutes later, this would not have happened to you. These feelings of guilt can quickly turn into self-blame which ultimately leads to feelings of depression. At this stage you may also experience a lack of or increase in your appetite, lack of energy – you don't feel like doing anything (like cleaning your home or spending time with your friends and family) heck, you may not even feel like washing your dirty behind! In fact, you may go into a state of intense withdrawal from everyone whom you know, which can ultimately affect you, family and friends.

Stage 4: Acceptance & Sharing

Once you reach the Acceptance & Sharing stage, you are finally admitting and telling the world that you have accepted your situation and are now ready to move forward. You then begin to reach out to your friends and family and share with them what's going on with you in hopes that they can help you with a plan or better yet, help you find a job.

At this stage you also feel a sense of relief, especially if your job had you overwhelmed and a bit stressed out. You may begin to look at your new found freedom as a blessing…perhaps something that needs to happen in order for you to reach the next stage in your career.

Recovering from a layoff is an arduous process. It's not something that you can recover from overnight. It is imperative to understand that everyone deals with lay-offs through the various stages in different time frames. Hey, you may have been fortunate to be able to bounce back from your layoff situation rather quickly. But for others, it can be a rather lengthy process to find another job. The truth is, everybody's experience is different. So always be understanding and supportive. Never pressure someone else to hurry up and bounce back.

You have to be patient with them. Just because you may see them eating bon-bons while watching television or headed out of town almost every weekend, doesn't mean that they aren't doing anything to help their situation. They could just still be at stage 1 or 3. The point is you never know what someone is actually going through, unless they tell you, and even then, they may not tell you everything.

TIP 3
GIVE YOURSELF TIME TO GRIEVE THE LOSS OF YOUR JOB.

Cue in the crying! Now, this is the time to cry. The important thing to do during your layoff is to grieve. Give yourself a few days to mourn the loss of your job. So you ask, "How do I mourn the loss of my job?" Well, that's easy. What you do is shut yourself down mentally and physically. What I mean is don't think about the job or anything else that is stressful. Veg out on the couch by watching non-thinking movies (I suggest comedies) or take time to go to the movies.

Use this time to spend by yourself. Of course, if you have a spouse or significant other or even children, take the opportunity to spend some quality time with them. Go shopping, sure you can't go crazy like you would normally, but buy yourself something pretty or buy a new gadget.

Perhaps you can get some travel time in and visit family and friends whom you haven't seen in awhile. Get some much needed rest and sleep in for a change. Work on those in-home projects that you have been neglecting which you didn't have time for because of your work schedule. Go to the gym, you know that you've been neglecting your body since you started working. This is the time to really focus on you - a time to re-evaluate your life and what you really want to do with your career. But remember, only give yourself about a week or less to grieve. You don't want to get so comfortable that you forget that you are back in the market for a new job. You want to get beyond relying on that weekly unemployment check. Additionally, you don't want to drive yourself into a habit of eating bon-bons and sitting on the couch for a living watching Victor Newman (from the Young and the Restless) in the same tight black t-shirt and jeans that he's been wearing since 1980.

In my case, once I filed for unemployment and grieved the loss of my fabulous one month career, I decided to do the next logical step. No, not pole dancing at the local strip club. Instead, I signed up with Randstad Staffing, a nationally known unemployment agency.

The most important step prior to registering for unemployment agencies is to update your resume. Make sure that your resume is clear, concise and relevant to the positions that you are applying for. Your re-

Kimberly C. Kisner

sume needs to sell your professionalism. In other words, you need to "brand" yourself. Because just like Coca Cola and Delta Air Lines are brands, so are you. Who can better market and sell themselves than you?

To Do List

1. Do grieve the loss of your job, but briefly.
2. Do make some time for yourself and your loved ones.
3. Do realize that recovery does not happen overnight.
4. Do register at unemployment agencies.
5. Do update your resume and "brand" yourself.

Kimberly C. Kisner

CHAPTER 4

THE JOB SEARCH

BY THIS TIME IN MY CAREER, I had only a few jobs on my resume that had anything to do with my Bachelors of Arts Degree in Mass Media Arts (Communications). So with that being the case, I arranged my resume in chronological order and updated my last position with the dates of my employment.

Unemployment agencies are really helpful in assisting you with finding temporary employment, to put money in your pocket, until you land a stable job. In fact, some of these temporary jobs can lead to full time permanent employment, especially if you are a good worker.

Now, keep in mind that these jobs usually pay by the hour so they may not be as lucrative as your last position. I was fortunate to obtain steady temporary work. My first temp position was with a national furniture store, in their home office, as a receptionist. I then worked for a national mortgage company in their home office, first as a receptionist and eventually I worked my way up to the HR department. Both jobs were pretty good and I gained some valuable work experience.

In addition to registering with local unemployment agencies, I conducted serious job searches on various well-known job sites such as Monster, Hotjobs, Careerbuilders, and local newspapers. Now, when you are searching on the various job sites, you have to be strategic, which brings me to Tip #4.

TIP 4
DON'T BE DESPEARTE IN YOUR JOB SEARCH.

Ok, I know, I know, you are in need of a job in a hurry. In my case, remember I told you that I was only awarded 2 weeks of severance pay? So this meant that I needed some additional income rather quickly. Sure unemployment was a mere $200 a week, but I still needed more to take care of all my bills. The key here is to not be desperate. Statistics show that once you have been laid off from your company, it typically takes anywhere from 3-6 months to find another gig. So with that being said, don't be like some people when they are looking for a relationship. Don't just settle for whatever comes your way, even if it's not what you are looking for. You have to be strategic in your job search. You have to think about the type of position you want, including location, salary, benefits and hours.

At this point in my career I wanted a job that was going to encompass all of my interest and talents as it relates to writing, communications, television and public relations etc. I only looked for jobs within the Advertising/Public Relations arena. This brings me back to my temp job at the mortgage company. Because I was such a good worker, they offered me a full-time position in their marketing department, but I ended up turning it down because I had another offer on the table, not to mention I had no interest in the area of marketing (that is until later in my career). Yep, I know you're wondering, "Wow that was fast!" How did that happen? It happened because I didn't just rely on the temp agencies to help me find a job. I continuously looked on the various job sites to find employment because finding a job is a job within itself. In the words of Sean "Puffy" Combs, "You can't stop, it won't stop!" you have to look every day. Of course, if you can't look every day, then definitely look every week.

As it turns out, I landed a temporary job working with one of the local airlines, with the possibility of being hired full-time in their Corporate Communications Department. This opportunity was a temp-to-perm position. I worked really hard and did my best. I was making a decent salary. In fact, I was making about $40,000 a year. That was excellent, considering at my last position, prior to me moving to Atlanta, I was making about $25- $30,000 a year (this was in Cleveland, Ohio at a local television station).

For the next 3 months, I worked hard trying to prove to my boss that I could do this job and finally all my work paid off. I was offered a permanent full-time position with the airline and even managed a promotion to Sr. Representative of Corporate Communications making $50,000 a year. Wow! I couldn't' believe it. I actually did it. I managed to land a job that I really liked within 4 months, just 2 months shy of the deadline that my mom gave me for having to move back home.

Now you're thinking, "What a happy ending to a story that started out not looking so promising as it related to Kim's career." Ha! Ha! The joke was on me because this was just the beginning for me!

After working for the airline for approximately 5 years, the inevitable happened. I'll never forget this day. Our company, of course, had been going through some financial difficulties. In fact, I managed to survive two earlier layoffs in the organization. However, since I knew another layoff was going to occur, I prepared better this time. On to Tip #5.

Kimberly C. Kisner

To Do List

1. Do not be ashamed of taking temporary positions – You never know where they might lead you.
2. Do search on various career Web sites.
3. Do not be desperate with your job search – You do not have to accept just ANY job because of your situation.
4. Do seriously think about the type of job YOU want.

CHAPTER 5

ANOTHER LAYOFF?

TIP 5
IF YOU HAVE KNOWLEDGE OF PENDING LAYOFF START PREPARING FOR YOUR EXIT FROM THE BUILDING SOONER THAN LATER.

IN THE CORPORATE WORLD, rumors usually do come true and you don't want to be caught out on a limb. If you hear whispers about a layoff, please don't think that you won't be affected. Fortunately, I made it through two layoffs prior to the third one, which affected me. I made sure that my resume was updated and all of the files that I could use in my electronic portfolio to get my next job were downloaded to a disc (Back then we used discs not USB ports).

Once I downloaded everything that I needed and packed my boxes, I began my next job search by getting my resume back out there, during my down time of course.

With this pending layoff dangling over my head, I felt a bit more confident about the situation and was more prepared this time. Since my resume was ready to go and I had already put out feelers for potential job prospects, I knew that finding another job would be a lot quicker for me because I began the process much sooner.

Smiling in the Face of Change!

So that fateful day finally arrived. I remember it just like it was yesterday. I came into work around 8:30 a.m. and logged onto my computer and began checking my e-mails. There were faint whispers in the hallway all morning…funny looks were on the faces of my peers. Then at approximately 10:00 a.m. my office phone rang. It was the vice president's Corporate Communications secretary summoning me to the upstairs conference room. Considering that I already had a feeling what was getting ready to happen in the conference room, I wasn't worried.

I got up and began my walk down the long hallway as though I was getting ready to go to the electric chair. My head was held high and my shoulders were upright and I was as smooth as could be. When I walked into the conference room I was greeted by my VP of Corporate Communications and the HR Manager for my area. The director was seated on the left and the HR Manager was seated on the right, and I was seated at the head of the table as though I was Joan Crawford in *Mommie Dearest* getting ready to greet the board members of Pepsi Co. There were loads of paper work on the table. The HR Manager handed me an official separation letter and explained to me in detail what was happening within our department.

Unlike my first lay-off experience, I listened very intently to everything that was being said - and I even had the nerve to have a smile on my face. I guess my smile must have been a tad bit annoying because my VP asked me, "Why are you smiling?" And in true Kim fashion I explained, " Why shouldn't I be smiling? Do you expect me to cry? There's nothing to cry about. I knew this day was coming and I had already prepared myself for this situation." Of course, he was perplexed and surprised by my brutal honesty. But really, there was nothing for me to cry about. I had to be a grown up and quickly accept my fate, whether I liked it or not.

TIP 6
ACCEPTANCE – YOU CAN'T CHANGE WHAT'S HAPPENING.

Ok I know that acceptance is mentioned in the part of the book that discusses grieving the loss of your job. But this point really needs reiterating, you need to grasp the concept and feeling of acceptance rather quickly. What I mean by that is you need to have an understanding of acceptance while you are in the room with HR and your boss. This tip works hand-in-hand with the, "Never Let Them See You Cry Tip." Like the Serenity prayer, "Lord grant me the wisdom to accept the things that I cannot change and the wisdom to know the difference." This is so true! Because the reality is that crying and making a scene will not change the situation. They will not see those crocodile tears running down your cheek and suddenly have a change of heart. Sorry it's not going to happen.

On the other hand, getting angry, cursing out your boss and the HR representative isn't necessary either. In fact, it's just downright unacceptable behavior. Instead of being escorted from the building gracefully, you may find yourself being escorted by the S.W.A.T team. Taking the high road and ACCEPTING what's happening to you is a more mature response to the situation. Because I repeat, you can't change the outcome once the decision is made.

Needless to say, I was a bit proud of myself during this particular layoff experience because I was confident and ACCEPTING and no tears rolled down my face. I deserved an Oscar for my stellar performance. Then of course, just like my first layoff experience, the HR representative informed me that they needed me to leave the building within the next hour. They said that I could make arrangements to retrieve the rest of my belongings later.

"Really? Again, what did they think I was going to do?" But little did they know, I had already begun taking some of my personal belongings home and I downloaded all of my files. There was no need for me to make arrangements to retrieve the rest of my belongings at a later time.

Per my commandment, I immediately went back to my office and gathered up all of my things and shut down my computer, turned in my lap top, keys and company credit card and was gracefully escorted out of the building.

I got into my car and drove around the parking lot for a bit and then I stopped the car…then to my surprise it happened. Yep, tears began to roll down my face. I was in a state of shock. I mean, I was with this company for 5 years and now I have no more job to go to in the mornings. However, after I calmed down and wiped away the tears, there was indeed a bright side to my situation. Because I was with the company for almost 5 years, I was entitled to receive 3-4 months of severance pay and on top of that I was able to keep my flight privileges for one year. And it gets even better, I planned on filing my taxes early so honestly, I knew that I was going to be Ok financially for at least 4-6 months provided that I stuck to a budget.

Now that I had accepted the fact that I no longer had a job to go to in the mornings, I began the grieving process. In this case, I didn't really need to take advantage of the full grieving process because I looked at this obstacle in my life as a stepping stone to something even greater. I used this time to relax, spend time with friends and to focus on my job search.

I contacted the staffing agencies and I reached out to all of my friends via e-mail to inform them of what just took place in my life and for them to keep their ears and eyes open for any available positions in my field. To my surprise, my networking with my friends paid off.

To Do List

1. Do not ever get too comfortable because your next layoff could be around the corner.
2. Do learn to accept the things that you cannot change and move forward.
3. Do not get angry and curse out your boss – it's not always their fault.
4. Do look at these obstacles as stepping stones to YOUR NEXT SUCCESS.

Kimberly C. Kisner

CHAPTER 6

MORE THAN JUST A MOBILE NETWORK

TIP 7
USE YOUR FRIENDS AS NETWORK OPPORTUNITIES.

AS DEFINED IN THE *WEBSTER DICTIONARY*, **networking** is "the exchange of information or services among individuals, groups, or institutions; specifically: the cultivation of productive relationships for employment or business." This is another way of finding your next employment opportunity. Networking should not just be limited to strangers, you should also engage in networking with your family and friends.

The first thing that you need to do is to communicate to your family and friends what just occurred. Of course, with modern technology you can pick up the phone and call them, send them a text message or shoot them an e-mail. You can also connect with friends, family and former co-workers on social networks such as, Facebook, LinkedIN and even Twitter. All of which are effective means of communicating. Your e-mail text message or phone message can go a little something like this:

Hello _____.

This is ###, how are you doing?

I'm doing ok, except for the fact that those DEMONS FROM HELL just laid me off yesterday!

Ok…I'm just kidding! You probably don't want to say that. Basically, you would say something like this:

Hello_____.

This is ###, how are you doing?

I'm doing ok, except for the fact that I was just laid off yesterday from _____.

Yes, I knew it was a possibility, but I'm going to be ok.

Hey, I was wondering if you could perhaps keep an eye out for any open positions in the area of _____ at your job or elsewhere. I would greatly appreciate it. I will forward my resume to you.

Great and thanks!

You see unlike networking with a perfect stranger at some mix or mingle event, your family and friends (most of them) have your best interest at heart. They will do whatever they can to help and support you. Believe me they want you to get another job so that you won't have to call and ask them for a loan.

Networking with my friends did turn out to be a very positive experience for me. I was actually attending a party and ran into an old friend. We talked about life and what was going on with each other. Of course, I informed him that I was recently laid off and was in the job market. We then exchanged phone numbers and he told me to call him. About a week later, while I was being a couch potato, I decided to give my old friend a call. We were engaging in light chit chat and then he informed me that his company was actually looking for someone, but the position was for a Marketing Specialist.

I was a bit unsure about this position seeing as though I had very little experience in marketing. Although I was in my last year of graduate school – finishing up my MBA in marketing - I really didn't have any hands-on experience with marketing, but I figured "What the heck?" I should at least apply for the position, especially since I had a friend who already worked at the company. He could perhaps put in a good word for me.

At his suggestion, I went to the company website and applied for the position immediately. From the job description, it looked like something that I could do, even though it was in the insurance industry, which of course is vastly different from the airline industry, and this position was dealing with external marketing communications with insurance agents and brokers. Thanks to my stellar resume, experience and with the help of my friend, I was able to land the Marketing Specialist position at the insurance company. However, landing this great job turned out not to be the best career move for me! You won't believe what happened next? Keep reading.

To Do List

1. Do utilize your Friends network to help land your next job.
2. Do get on the various Social Networks – They're not just for status updates of your life!
3. Do not be afraid of a challenge - just because you may not be the most experienced in that field does not mean you will not get the job.

Kimberly C. Kisner

CHAPTER 7

STOP...WAIT A MINUTE...SELF-INFLICTED LAYOFF

UP UNTIL NOW FOLKS, I've been talking to you about what happens when you get laid off from a company and how you should handle that obstacle. I'm afraid that there's another layoff that I must talk to you about. It's called the *self-inflicted layoff*. Yes, that's right, a self-inflicted layoff. This is when, due to no fault of the organization, one puts themselves in a position in which they decide to leave a company abruptly, usually without having another job waiting for them in the wings.

This is exactly what happened to me. I couldn't leave this part of my life out of the book because I learned some very valuable lessons that helped to catapult me to my next job. I also couldn't leave this part out of the book because my experience could be used to guide you in case you find yourself teetering on the dark side of a self-inflicted layoff.

Working at the insurance corporation taught me a lot about people, working relationships and politics within Corporate America. Have you ever been in a situation where you felt like you weren't being appreciated? Or in a situation where your boss was jealous and intimated because of your education and experience? Well, that's the jest of what happened to me.

I was in a situation where I wasn't respected professionally and personally by my female bosses. However, in retrospect I probably could have played the "corporate political game" a little bit better. I'm sure as many of you know, playing that game can be tiresome and not worth the hassle. At this point in my career, I just knew if I did a good job, got to know the right people, applied a good work ethic and always gave 100 percent that I would be promoted. But that strategy didn't work.

Apparently, I didn't play the game as well as I thought. You all know what I'm referring too right? Some will define the corporate game in the workplace as the "calculated means of getting things done." Unfortunately, it is also a way that people twist and turn situations to reach a specific goal, usually a goal that is all about "self." The downside of the corporate game is that those who don't play, risk their careers. In my case, that's exactly what happened.

It is often said, as it relates to the corporate world, "If you improperly manage the power and politics of your corporate culture, you could cause a dent in your career," which will cause stress - another thing that happened to me. Don't get me wrong, not excelling at the insurance company was not due to lack of skill or intelligence, it was simply because I chose to be my own person and not conform to the cultural politics at my workplace.

I had a (bad) habit of always speaking my mind, no matter what. However, I can admit, that at times my speaking out wasn't as tactful and respectful as it could have been, even though my reasons for speaking out were valid. You see, there's nothing wrong with speaking up for what you believe in or protecting your character and integrity never the less, it's important that you always do it with tact, diplomacy and class.

Think about the 2008 presidential election when then Senator Obama

Kimberly C. Kisner

Laid Off But NOT Laid Out

and Senator McCain debated one another. No matter what Senator McCain threw at President Obama, he always maintained diplomacy and class and responded as cool as a cucumber. President Obama stood up for what he believed in without getting emotionally aroused.

So yes, even though I didn't always handle my work situations in the best way, I can tell you the one thing that I did do right was keep a journal of every conversation and a record of all e-mails that occurred with my boss, as well as any unfair situations that I was part of. I stood my ground for as long as I could, until one day everything came to a head - lies were being thrown and false accusations were being tossed back-and-forth via e-mail between me, my bosses, and Human Resources.

As you can probably guess, I just couldn't take it anymore. So on a crisp sunny November day, I called everyone who was close to me to ask for guidance as to how I should handle this situation, but for some reason, no one appeared to answer their phones. As a result, I did the only thing possible. That's right, I went outside into the elements and let the sun hit my face and the wind blow a soft breeze on my cheek. Then I closed my eyes and said a little prayer to God: "God, please help me. What should I do?" And in that brief moment with Him, I got my answer. Yes! He works just that fast. God is indeed Good all the time.

Although I didn't realize what his answer was until I got back upstairs to my desk. I sat down at my desk very calmly. I wrote out my resignation letter, I deleted all of my e-mails and important files. I packed up all of my personal items from the desk drawer. I then logged off my computer, grabbed my office sweater and bag and then went into my boss's office. I laid down my letter of resignation on top of her desk without saying a word to her, and then I calmly turned around and walked out of her office. She called herself semi-chasing me down the hallway to get me to change my mind, and all I said to her was, "You should have thought about that before you started all of this!" And then

Kimberly C. Kisner

without losing a step, I got on the elevator and left the building.

Once I left the building, I got into my car and drove off feeling like I was Rosa Parks – not allowing anyone to push me around and have to give up my seat on the bus. Yep. I was a hero to myself and others who suffer from Corporate America injustice - that is until reality set in. "Oh my God, I just quit my job! I have a mortgage to pay, car note and other bills. And I have no other job waiting for me in the wings. What am I going to do?" This of course brings me to tip #8:

TIP 8
DON'T QUIT YOUR JOB UNLESS YOU HAVE ANOTHER ONE.

Don't get the wrong impression. I don't regret for a minute what I did. You see, if you are in a situation that is getting the best of you - where you find yourself dreading to get up in the morning to go to work - then it's time for a change. However, change doesn't necessarily happen overnight. So I suggest you be strategic in how you are going to handle your situation. Like I said, "I don't regret what I did," but if I had just stayed a little while longer and let the games play out, financially I would have come out much better. But struggling the way I did made me a stronger person and strengthened my faith in God.

I knew that I wouldn't be in my jobless situation much longer. In fact, while I was working at the insurance company, I did submit my resume to other job openings and I did happen to have two interviews at one particular company prior to me leaving the insurance company, but I had no idea how that situation was going to turn out.

Well, one day as I was driving in my car realizing that I would not be receiving direct deposits from a job anymore, I called my parents. Even though I was thirty-something, I was a bit nervous about telling my parents that I resigned from my job without having a back-up job. Fortunately, both of my parents were aware of my difficulties at work so they were both pretty supportive and empathetic to my plight *(Side Note: They would have to be, since I was going to need some financial support from both of them)*.

To my surprise, my parents were proud of me for doing what I did. They told me that it took guts to step out there on faith and take a risk. I told them about my conversation with God and how I knew that this was something that I had to do – no, in fact that I needed to do. So I did it!

Oh and did I mention that at the time of my sudden departure, my younger brother was living with me? Yep, and I wasn't charging him any rent because he was trying to get himself established and on track professionally as he just graduated from college. And, here is the kicker: it's like Christmas in Spring time! (But not really) Not only was I out of a job, but the very next day, my beloved younger brother was laid off from his job. **(*Side Note: He had only been working for about a month or so and he wouldn't be receiving any SEVERANCE PAY.*)** When he came home and told me that, we both cracked up laughing because here we were living in a house and we had bills to pay, but neither one of us had jobs. CLASSIC! It doesn't get any better than this.

My emancipation from the insurance company occurred right before Thanksgiving and soon after that came Christmas. Thank God for the mother that I have because she wanted to make sure that her children came home for Christmas, so she purchased airplane tickets for the both of us.

While we were home for Christmas, I got an early Christmas gift. I received a call from the hiring manager of the company where I had been interviewing over the last month or so while I was still working at the insurance company. They wanted to hire me! I was so excited about this opportunity. I was going to be the Communications Manager for the Hu-

Kimberly C. Kisner

man Resources department. However, I wouldn't be able to start work until Jan. 15. But hey, I didn't care because I was going to be employed after being out of work for about a month. Not bad for someone who resigned from her job without having another job waiting in the wings.

As for my brother, well he took the networking approach (tip #7) and was in steady communication with our cousin who was an executive at a charter school in Maryland. After a few months of talking and a few interviews, my brother landed a job in Maryland as a teacher. Of course that meant he had to move from Hotlanta and head to Maryland. Even though I was sad to see him go, I was ecstatic that he got a job and we were both getting back on our feet professionally and financially.

TIP 9
IF YOU'RE NOT HAPPY WITH YOUR CURRENT JOB, START LOOKING FOR SOMETHING ELSE DURING YOUR DOWN TIME.

One of the reasons why I was only out of work for about two months is because I had already begun my job search several months in advance of resigning. You see, my original plan was to have a job offer on the table and then resign from the insurance company. However, God had another plan for me. My advice to you is that if you aren't feeling satisfied or challenged in your current position, then it is in your best interest to put some feelers out there. Upload your resume on the various job sites and begin your job search early. But remember, only look for another job during your down time at home, not while you're at work. You don't want to get fired because you were caught looking on job sites during work hours.

Kimberly C. Kisner

To Do List

1. Do learn the "Corporate" game, but don't lose who you are while learning it.
2. Do speak your mind but do it with tact and diplomacy.
3. Do keep a record of e-mails and conversations, you may need them to prove a point or to defend yourself.
4. Do not quit your current job until you have another one waiting in the wings.

CHAPTER 8

JUST WHEN I THOUGHT IT WAS SAFE

JANUARY 15, 2008 (MARTIN LUTHER KING'S HOLIDAY) was my first day at my new job. Even though, I was perhaps the only person that I knew who had to go to work on this day, I didn't care. Heck, I had been on unemployment vacation for the last two months. I was ready to hit the ground running in Corporate America again. This was one of the best jobs I had gotten since working at the airlines.

My new boss was great; she wasn't a micro-manager. She trusted me and gave me freedom. I had flexible work hours and I had the ability to work from home at times. Additionally, there was a cafeteria on campus where I could get free breakfast and lunch every day. Ok maybe not free. The cost was about $5.00 a month out of my paycheck. Who could beat that? Considering how much it would normally cost to purchase lunch every day. Also, there was an indoor workout facility and bowling alley. I never used the bowling alley, but I did use the workout equipment.

The company that I was working for was on a roll. We were acquiring other companies and things were looking very promising for me career wise. I was heading up several projects and making new friends.

Kimberly C. Kisner

Everything was going rather smoothly. After about six or seven months into my position things took a drastic turn. It appears that one of our competitors who was much larger than the company I worked for, decided to acquire us.

You know what that means right? Whenever you have a merger or acquisition, there are almost always layoffs. Of course, the company announced to all of the employees that there was going to be some restructuring, that's code for layoffs. But I did not panic. Of course, some of my colleagues were panicking and getting nervous; but I, on the other hand, was not nervous because I was a pro when it came to layoffs. I did what I knew I needed to do. I began my job search by putting feelers out there, just in case I was one of the employees who would be dismissed.

As a Communications Manager, I was privy to information as it related to the pending acquisition and restructuring. I must be honest I figured that I was needed and I definitely wasn't going to be one of the first people to be laid off. Additionally, I had a few key contacts within the Human Resources department and they assured me that if there was a layoff, especially in my department they would let me know in advance.

Mind you, I didn't ask this person to give me that information, she volunteered. You do know what volunteered means right? Well, apparently my contact in the HR department didn't really mean what she said. I knew that my friend would keep me in the know, and if I was going to be laid off, I would know sooner than later.

One day during the week, I can't remember exactly what day it was, but a few of us decided to go out to lunch. Included in this lunch group, was my friend (and I use that term loosely) who said she would keep me in the know, another friend who had once been with the company but had resigned a few months back, and one other co-worker from HR. This lunch was really a time for all of us to catch up. My friend who was no longer with the company was aware of the pending layoff situation and was naturally concerned for all of us. So while we were waiting for our food to arrive, she asked my HR "friend" if she knew if I was going to be losing my job. She looked all of us in the eye, and with a straight face said, "No, I don't have that information. I only have numbers."

Then my friend said, "Well, do you know approximately how many people from Kim's group will be losing their jobs?" And she replied, "No, I don't have that information."

During this entire conversation, I remained silent because I didn't want to remind her that she did volunteer to keep me posted. On top of that, she worked in the Payroll Department of HR and would most certainly know before I did who was going to be laid off. Being the trustworthy friend that I am, I believed her. So, I just assumed that I had nothing to worry about, because I KNEW she had my back. Therefore, I felt like I could breathe a little easier.

The next day, I went to work as usual and I noticed that it was a bit quieter than normal. I was in my usual upbeat mood, and honestly, I didn't really have a whole lot on my plate. In fact, for the past month or so my workload was rather sparse. I was at work for about an hour and a half before my boss came to my desk and said that she wanted to see me to discuss a project with her in about 30 minutes. I of course said, "OK!"

Thirty minutes finally came and my boss came to get me, she said, "We are going to discuss the project upstairs in the Vice President's office."

"What?" I thought to myself. That really didn't make any sense to me. Why did we need to discuss a project upstairs on executive row? Especially, since I knew that the VP was on vacation. Something was definitely up and it wasn't good.

My boss and I walked in the VP's office and guess who was in the office waiting for us? That's right, the VP of HR with a folder and paper work. This scene looked familiar to me. I've been down this road before. My boss and I sat down, and I sat next to the VP of HR. I couldn't believe my eyes; I couldn't believe what was about to take place, yet AGAIN! I mean, I had only been in this position one year. In fact, I was a few days shy from my one year anniversary –no special gift for me.

Anyway, my boss looked a bit misty eyed. I actually thought that she was going to start crying. She looked so distraught and hurt, that I had to keep my composure because I didn't want her to feel bad. As luck would have it, my company was laying me off. I was going to be on the books until February, after that I would receive about three to four months of severance pay. Well, I signed the papers with my head held high and a smile on my face. My boss and I left out of the office and she walked me back to my desk. She kept apologizing and saying how much she was going to miss me and gave me her personal phone numbers and e-mail address and asked me to please stay in touch.

This time I was allowed to pack up some of my things, but I had to come back on that Friday prior to the offices being opened to get the rest of my belongings. As I gathered up my box of stuff and walked out to my car, I was in total disbelief. I couldn't believe this seriously was not happening to me again. I got into my car and drove away from yet another company. I made my usual calls to give the bad news. I called my parents and they were both a bit shocked, but as usual they were very supportive. I guess I wasn't safe; I guess my HR friend really didn't have my back after all.

After I was released from my wonderful job, I really couldn't be that upset because as I mentioned earlier, work in my area was becoming scarce which caused me to experience a small amount of boredom and discontent. I mean, there's only so much surfing on the Web and talking on the phone to your friends that I could do. I was at a point in my career where I didn't feel like I was being challenged enough and the lack of work didn't make it any better for me.

Most folks may enjoy the fact that they aren't being challenged or don't have a lot on their plates in terms of work. This of course, would give them freedom to roam the Internet or catch up on the latest gossip with their friends and family. However, since getting out of my twenties my work ethic has improved. I don't enjoy just talking on the phone with my friends while I'm at work– hopefully they don't have time to talk either because they too have jobs.

Ok I got off track for a minute. But like I was saying, I really couldn't be that upset about being laid off because unlike most people, I had a fall back position. What was my fall back? Glad you asked. In addition to my full time job, I also had a part time job. Tip #10.

TIP 10
HAVE A FALL BACK – GET A PART TIME JOB!

Having a fall back as it relates to another job to supplement your income from your full time place of employment is a key element to surviving a layoff. I know you're probably thinking, "I don't have time for another job?" Well, I do understand that, but if you have some time perhaps a few evenings out of the week or maybe over the weekend, a part time job may be able to fit into your schedule. It is important to do your research and find part-time job opportunities that will suite you and your financial needs. Ok, back to the regularly schedule program…..

You see I was the Director of Marketing at my church. This job was really great. Aside from earning extra income for my pockets, it allowed me the freedom to work from home most of the time. Additionally, it was also a challenge for me because this was the first time that my

Kimberly C. Kisner

church had a marketing department. I basically had to build the department from the ground up. I must admit, even though it was a part time job it was a lot of work, and to be honest, it was hard to juggle my part time gig with my regular work schedule.

You see, normally when people think about getting a part time job, they opt for a job that doesn't involve a lot of strategic thinking and time – the job is usually a no brainer type. You know, one that doesn't involve a lot of thought or creativity etc.

So why did I choose to get a part time job that involved the same skills that I used during my day job? That's easy to answer. I really enjoy marketing/communications. That's what I went to school for. But the job at the church was a bit different than working in Corporate America.

First of all, the church was a place that was very familiar with me. I had been a member there for about 8 years, so I knew a lot of people and they knew me. I had somewhat of an idea of how I could utilize my skills to help enhance the marketing presence of my church and I really wanted to see if I could assist in any way.

Now, obtaining the Director of Marketing position at the church was not that easy. It took about 6 months before I actually got the job. I went through several interviews and had to submit samples of my work and actually put together a marketing plan for the church. Thankfully, my pastor and key staff members thought that I was a good fit for the position.

For the next four months, after being laid-off from my full-time job, I was working full time hours but being paid a part time salary. That was okay though, because I figured if I showed my dedication and worked really hard, I would be asked to be full time rather quickly. Ok, actually I tried very hard to convince or rather persuade them to hire me in a full time capacity - meaning, working full time hours and receiving full time pay.

Well, while I was waiting to see if I was going to be hired on a full time basis, I had to figure out a way to supplement my income. Remember, I had only received about four months severance from my other job. So, since I was laid off in January, my severance wouldn't run out until about June and I couldn't file for unemployment until my severance ran out. On top of having severance until June, I filed my taxes early. This meant that my finances were pretty stable because I took my nice size income tax check and deposited it directly into my savings account, so I wouldn't spend it all.

TIP 11

IF YOU CAN FILE YOUR TAXES EARLY... THE EXTRA INCOME CAN HELP OFF-SET YOUR UNEXPECTED LOSE OF INCOME!

The great thing about income tax time is that you can file early and get your refund back to you before the April 15 tax deadline. Ok, let me restate that comment: The great thing about tax season (if you don't owe the IRS) is that you can file early and get your refund back way before the April 15 deadline. Filing your income taxes early is a great way to supplement your income until you get back on your feet. However, the key is that you MUST put your money into your savings account so that you don't misspend it.

I'm sure there are plenty of wonderful things that you want to do with your extra money. You probably would like to take that trip to the islands or purchase hard wood floors in your kitchen – oh that's what I wanted to do with my money, but you get the idea. Unfortunately, life sometimes throws us a wrench in even the best made plans. So instead of taking a trip to the islands or getting hardwood floors for your kitchen, you can use this money to pay your mortgage, rent or any other bills that you may have. Trust me, you will be glad that you didn't blow your entire income tax check splurging on the finer things in life.

Back to the story.....

When my severance finally ran out, I had forgotten the fact that I did not file for unemployment. One of my girlfriends who was laid off, said to me, "Girl, just because it's May doesn't mean that you can't go and file for your unemployment."

"But I was laid off back in January!" I exclaimed. My friend replied, "So, you can still file for it. You better go and get your money!"

I took my friends advice and filed for unemployment immediately. By working full time (making part time money) collecting unemployment, and still having some of the money I had from my tax refund, I was ok for a minute. Then in June, I received great news. The church decided to bring me onboard in a full time capacity. This great news meant that I could no longer accept my unemployment benefits. And that was OK, because I was making a decent salary. So everything was fabulous in my world, or so I thought.

To Do List

1. Do put out "feelers" when you hear rumors of mergers, acquisitions and layoffs.
2. Do not trust everyone in your company –everyone does not have your best interest in mind.
3. Do have multiple streams of income, like a part-time job.
4. Do file for unemployment as soon as possible.

Kimberly C. Kisner

CHAPTER 9

OH MY...NOT AGAIN!

ABOUT A MONTH INTO MY FULL-TIME POSITION, we had a staff meeting to discuss the church's financial situation. It wasn't the fact that our members weren't paying tithes or giving offerings, but the staff was spending more money than we were bringing into the church.

You see, our pastor had warned us several months before about the church's spending, and as a result, he told us that there was going to be a freeze on the staffing budget. He also stated that we needed to curtail our spending or other cost-cutting measures would have to take place.

Unfortunately, the staff didn't adhere to the pastor's warning. At our regularly scheduled staff meeting a few months later, the pastor told us that there would be some layoffs within our organization and that no one was exempt. I have to be honest though. My ego got in the way and I really didn't think that my position would be in jeopardy because, in my opinion, how could the church get rid of me...the Marketing Director? My position was definitely a necessity.

None the less, just as the pastor said, there were layoffs. It was unbelievable! One of my direct reports was laid off; a receptionist was laid off and a few other part time staff members were let go. Watching this occur,

I still didn't think that I would be laid off. The whole layoff process was interesting because our HR Manager was a part time employee and he didn't make it into the office that often. So, whenever he came into the office, we knew something was up. We knew that it must be serious if he was in the office. On this particular Friday, he was running around - going back and forth to the copy and fax machine and in and out of his office with the door closed. Everyone in the office was a bit nervous, but I wasn't that nervous because if they let me go, who would handle the marketing?

Well, it wouldn't be me as I was going to soon find out. As I said, on this particular Friday, the HR Manager was running around the office handling his business and he came by my desk and said, "I'm going to need to see you in a few minutes? Will you be available?" Of course I said, "Yes."

I honestly didn't' know why he wanted to see me because the last time I was in his office, he informed me that the church was going to lay off one of my direct reports and he wanted me to know first. So, I couldn't imagine why he needed to see me unless he was planning to lay off my other direct report.

A few minutes passed and sure enough, the HR Manager said, "Are you ready?" and I said, "Sure."

I went into his office with a pen and notebook in case I needed to take notes or something. Come to find out, the only note that I needed to take was, "I'm laid off yet again…twice in one year!

I thought, "What the hell?!" That's why he wanted to see me in his office. He wanted to inform me that the church was laying me off, but here was the kicker, if the budget happened to turn around in two months (you see I was laid off in July) then I would be asked to come back. Yeah, like that was really going to happen. *(Side Note: It never hap-*

Kimberly C. Kisner

pened)

Even though I was being laid off in July, they kept me on the books until mid September. So I did think that was generous. I was shocked to say the least. This had to be a joke, I knew that God had a sense of humor, but was he for real? I was laid off in January and now I'm laid off again in July. I really wasn't prepared for this. I was very angry about the situation. Words could not express how I was feeling - Ok, I'm lying; words could express how I was feeling.

I just couldn't believe that I was laid off from my church. I mean, I worked really hard and did a good job (so I thought) as the Director of Marketing. I have to be honest, my first thought was that there were other people there who I knew didn't work as hard as I did and yet they were still there (Again, my ego got in the way). However, I had to let those thoughts go because those individuals were apparently still needed and had been working at the church for a lot longer than me. But again, I was really angry.

I was angry at the pastor; I was angry at the HR Manager; and I was angry at myself. Why was Kim angry at Kim? Because when I was laid off from my full time job back in January, I immediately tried to convince the pastor, the CFO and the HR Manager to bring me onboard full time. I did this negotiating and convincing for about six months. Each month I thought it was going to happen, but it never did. I kept trying to force the issue, but with no success - at least not until six months later in June. I wasted time putting in all of those full time hours and not being paid as a full time employee. I could have or rather should have been looking for another full time job (when the economy wasn't as bad) but I didn't do that. I was so confident that I was going to be brought onboard as a full time employee immediately. And once I was a full time employee, I was laid off less than a month later.

Kimberly C. Kisner

As you can see, I had a lot to be upset about. I don't know if you are a believer in the will of God, and I believe in God whole-heartedly, although sometimes it's hard for me to grasp the concept of God's will for us. So with that being said, I understand that when what I'm doing is aligned with God's will, I feel a certain amount of peace. I also feel that things fall right into place without force.

You know, it's like when you are trying to make that relationship work with that man or woman and it's just not falling into place, you try to force a relationship, but it just doesn't seem to work out. That's probably a good indication that the relationship is not supposed to work. However, that's exactly what I was trying to do; force a relationship between me and the church to work full time instead of "resting in the will of God" and being satisfied with working part time.

Here's the thing, there's nothing wrong with being aggressive and trying to make something happen, but after a certain amount of time has gone by and no progress has been made, perhaps it's best to just move on. I didn't do that. What I should have done was work my part time job at the church while looking for a full time job. Needless to say, this is why I was a bit angry with myself. My anger prevented me from attending church service because I was too upset and plus a bit embarrassed.

As I mentioned earlier, I had been a member for eight years and people knew me and I knew them. I wanted to avoid any question like, what happened, you're not the Director of Marketing anymore? Plus, I needed some time to get over my anger. As a result, I stayed away from church for about two months and got over the angry and sad feelings.

I ended up making my return to my church the weekend of my birthday. I felt that would be a great time to go back to church, I couldn't celebrate another year of life without thanking God. I also thought it would be a good time for me to show my face without the embarrassing feelings that I felt internally because I was no longer employed with the church. I have to admit that it was uncomfortable being at the church after being away for two months, but it did feel good to be back in the house of the Lord. And I was able to be attentive to my pastor when he spoke, as opposed to allowing my anger to drown out his every word.

To Do List

1. Do not let your "Ego" get in the way of your career.
2. Do not try to keep forcing "your will" – It can be anything from a job to your personal life, if it's meant to be it will happen.
3. Do not get so comfortable that you forget about your ultimate career goals and dreams.

Kimberly C. Kisner

CHAPTER 10

OUT OF TWO JOBS...NOW WHAT?

LAID OFF TWICE IN ONE YEAR, now what was I to do? The economy was bad and jobs were not very plentiful. In fact, according to the US Labor Department the unemployment rate in 2008 hovered at 7.1%. Additionally, during the month of September 2008, employers cut a higher-than-expected 159,000 jobs. Not only was that more than double the layoffs during the months of July and August, but it was also the worst decline since 2003, when the economy was still in the throes of recession. And if this information wasn't hard enough to hear, in the state of Georgia the unemployment rate rose to 7.5 percent in November 2008. *(Side note: By the summer of 2009, Georgia's unemployment rate was 10.2 percent)*

Unemployment was the highest rate in more than 25 years. In fact, the rate climbed a full three percentage points from the previous year, when it was 4.5 percent. It was 6.9 percent in October. Georgia's jobless rate was running above the national rate, which was 6.7 percent for several months. More than 300,000 Georgians were looking for work and I was part of that shocking number. I was a statistic.

Kimberly C. Kisner

As you can see this situation was not good for me at all. By this time, I had depleted my savings and I only had until September to receive a payroll check from the church. Once the month of September rolled by, Kim was not going to have any money. Ok, maybe I'm being a bit dramatic. I wasn't without any money, I was receiving a weekly unemployment check, but that was about it.

This was a situation that may look familiar to you, but it was a bit different. I've never been laid off twice in one year. This was a serious low point in my life. I was really feeling scared this time. I had no more savings. I had to go into my scarce 401K and use that money to pay bills. I just couldn't wrap my mind around my situation. It was like some kind of dream. All I could think about was how I would make it and pay my bills each month:

Mortgage	= $1059
Car Note	= $462
Association Fee	= $185
Car/House Insurance	= $160
Medical Insurance	= $127
Utilities (Gas, Electricity)	= $75
Cable	=$75
Cell phone	=$100
Groceries	=$80
Entertainment	=varies
Grand Total (Approximately)	**= $2,323**

My weekly unemployment check was only $320.00 a week, which amounts to $1280.00 a month. You do the math. It just wasn't enough to cover my bills. Where was I going to get the rest of the money to support myself? On top of that, I was in fear of losing my house and having the repo man come and take away my car.

You see, I am naturally a person who tends to worry in troubled times, I'm also a person who thinks ahead. This characteristic is good for some situations, but not all. My mind was working overtime trying to figure out how to handle my situation. I honestly didn't want to ask my parents for help for the simple fact that they have both made so many sacrifices in their lives so their children could have certain things. Plus, I just have a hard time asking for help. I'm a person who strives to make it happen on my own, by being resourceful and thinking through things very carefully. Sometimes I've had to rob Peter to pay Paul, but I've done what I've had to do to survive.

To Do List

1. Do realize that it's ok to worry, you are human.
2. Do keep track of your monthly bills, so you can determine how to handle the shortfalls.
3. Be resourceful and prudent with your finances.

Kimberly C. Kisner

CHAPTER 11

I'M A SURVIVOR...I'M NOT GONNA GIVE UP!

I DIDN'T HAVE A CHOICE, I had to accept the fact that I was financially starving and job challenged at this point in my life and I needed to decide what my response was going to be to my situation. Was I going to curl up into the fetal position and rock myself back and forth? Or was I going to be proactive and "Find a Way or Make a Way?" **(Clark Atlanta school motto)**

Of course, I decided on the latter. I did what I hope you will do. I took my advice for surviving a layoff, and accelerated the pace, because this time I didn't have three to four months of severance pay to work with. Time was of the essence. I used my unemployment time to really focus on what it was that I wanted to do with my life.

I've always had an entrepreneurial spirit, except I just didn't know what I wanted to do. I knew that I had a passion for marketing and communications, but how could I use that passion to leverage my own business?

I decided to start my own marketing company. I had a little bit of extra money that I used to purchase a business license and registered with the Department of Labor. I had a friend who was a graphics artist who helped me design a logo free of charge. Once I got the logo designed, I was on my way to ordering and purchasing my company business cards. I was all set. Except, the fact that I didn't have a Web site nor did I have any money to have a Web site built. This is where you see the wonderful blessings that God has for us, but only if we have faith in his guidance.

One beautiful sunny Sunday afternoon, I was job hunting at one of my favorite spots: Starbucks. I had decided to be proactive with my job situation and take the want ads from the *Atlanta Journal Constitution* and look for a gig while sipping on an iced café mocha. To my surprise, I had no idea that I was being watched. No, not in a creepy stalker way. But there was a gentleman who was sitting across from me watching me while I was going through the paper. He then boldly got up from his seat to approach me and said, "Hello. I'm sorry to bother you, but I noticed you looking through the want ads. What type of job are you looking for?"

Now believe me, when he came up to my table, I was a bit suspicious of this strange man approaching me. However, he did seem very sincere. We engaged in polite conversation, and, as luck would have it, he and his business partner were looking for someone to handle the marketing/communications for their company. I, of course, was elated. I told him a little about myself, my job history and that I recently started my own marketing company and I was looking for clients. Well, that brief conversation turned into the scheduling of a meeting for later that week to discuss details.

"Wow!" I thought to myself, my first client. I couldn't believe it. No, yes I could because everything happens for a reason and it's also about timing.

Kimberly C. Kisner

Later that week, I met with my first client and we discussed his business and what he needed from me. Again, as fate would have it I mentioned to him how I was in need of a Web site for my company. He and his partner were in the business of building Web sites and we discussed a barter arrangement. I waived my retainer fee in exchange for his company building and hosting my Web site for a year. Because of my client, my business was official: first business cards and now a Web site, I was on my way to financial stability - at least so I thought.

Once I got the Web site up and running, I had my graphics artist design some direct mail postcards so that I could mail them to small businesses and organizations that I thought may be in need of marketing support. As a result of my postcards, I was able to rustle up a few more clients. In total I had about six clients.

Now my company wasn't bringing in a lot of revenue, but it did bring in enough to help me survive financially during my layoff period. So here I was getting a $320 a week unemployment check and I had a business on the side. I was doing pretty well for myself. However, I was still having some difficulties paying some of my bills, especially my mortgage. So needless to say, I was afraid that I would lose my house. My business wasn't doing that well, so where in the world would I get the money? Because I'm not one to ask for help, I decided to put my job search in high gear.

I not only applied for jobs in the Marketing/Communications field, but I also applied for any and every job I could think of. For example, administrative work, call centers, eye companies, drug stores etc. I knew that I had to do something because the unemployment checks and my business weren't going to produce enough revenue to sustain me. I was in overdrive looking for a job, I just knew that something was going to come up rather quickly.

Kimberly C. Kisner

I was fortunate to be able to make it to a few interviews, but most of the organizations looked at my resume and then looked at me, and would say, "You have an MBA. Why do you want to work here?"

"Umm… excuse me?" would be going through my head, "I know I have an MBA, but I'm in need of a job and I will learn and do whatever it takes."

Unfortunately, for me, that wasn't good enough. Most of the organizations were probably afraid to hire me because they were not sure if I would be there for the long-term. I really tried hard to find a job, any job. However, my phone was just not ringing. Well, it was ringing but on the other end there was usually a bill collector of some sort. I was at a standstill; I didn't know where I was going to be able to get extra money to pay some of my bills, especially the important one…my mortgage. This brings me to my next tip.

TIP 12
LEARN TO PUT YOUR PRIDE ASIDE AND DON'T BE AFRAID TO ASK FOR HELP.

This tip is essential to making it during a down time. You must learn to put your pride aside and ask for support. And if you are like me and have family who are willing to help you, then you are really blessed. There are a lot of individuals out there who don't have support from family and friends. I, of course, had to let go of my pride and make a few phone calls.

I sent my parents a break down of all of my monthly bills so they could see and understand what I was dealing with on a monthly basis. Once they saw the breakdown of my bills, they both pitched in every month to help me pay my mortgage and my other bills. Believe me I

Kimberly C. Kisner

knew that asking them for help wasn't in their financial plans every month, but I didn't have anywhere else to go. And I was truly grateful for all of their support.

To Do List

1. Do decide on how you are going to handle your situation – will you crawl up in a ball or be pro-active?
2. Do think about starting your own company.
3. Do not be afraid to apply for jobs that you may be over qualified for – Hey, sometimes you have to do what is necessary for survival.
4. Do not be afraid to ask for help – that's what a support system is for.

Kimberly C. Kisner

CHAPTER 12

FRIENDSHIP AND MONEY

TIP 13
KNOW WHO YOUR "REAL" FRIENDS ARE AND ALWAYS BE A "REAL FRIEND" YOURSELF.

DURING THE SEVEN MONTHS OR SO of being laid off, I was fortunate to have a wonderful group of friends who helped me through the rough times. People always say that you find out who your friends really are through adversity. Well, most of my friends definitely passed the test. *(Side Note: Friends, I really wasn't testing you, that is just a figure of speech)*

I remember I was talking to one of my friends over the phone and we were discussing life and how blessed we both were and how no matter what you are going through things could always be worse. During, our in-depth and profound conversation, he went on to say, "If you ever needed a bill or two to be paid, let me know and I will pay it."

I told him thank you, but I just knew that even though I had quite a few bills that needed to be taken care of, I just couldn't form my lips to ask him for help. That is until about a week or two later when my water was going to be shut-off unless I paid my bill. Once again, I had to let go of my pride and call up my friend and ask him for help. He did exactly what he promised. He paid my bill for me...and there were no strings attached.

On another occasion, I happened to be on Facebook and one of my college girlfriends and I were communicating via instant messenger and she happened to ask how I was doing? I was honest and told her that I was struggling a bit, but that I was going to be fine. She then offered to send some money to help ease my financial stress. I told her, the reason I didn't reveal to her what was going on with me was because I was not expecting to get any money from her. She said that it was not an issue to give me money because she remembered how I helped her out back in college when she needed a place to stay for the school year. Wow! I couldn't believe that she even remembered that, I almost forgot that myself. A few days later, I received a check in the mail from my friend.

Another friend, who I've only known for maybe less than a year, offered me money so that I could buy groceries. I told her that I couldn't take it, but she insisted and reminded me that friends help friends when they are in need. To my surprise, when I saw her at the next GNO (Girls Night Out) get together, she handed the money to me very discreetly in my hand so that no one else would have to know she was lending a helping hand in my time of need.

There have also been many times when I have gone out with my friends to dinner, breakfast, the movies etc. and my female and male friends have all treated me; paying for my movie ticket, my meal and of course a few drinks here and there. But let me ask you this, what do you do when you swallow your pride and ask your friend for help because you are in a financial abyss and they say they are going to help you out, and then renege on their commitment? Folks, that's what happened to me on several occasions.

Kimberly C. Kisner

I had a few friends whom I reached out to for help and they said that they would help me. One friend (who lived out of town) went so far as to even ask me for my home mailing address so that he could send me a little something. Folks, I'm still waiting for that little something in the mail.

And this next friend, who said they would help me really shocked, hurt and disappointed me. At the time, we had been friends for about ten years. And I might add, this friend is doing pretty well financially. Now, I have NEVER asked this person for help, but this time I was really in need and did not want to go to my parents again considering how they have already sacrificed so much for me. So, I went to my so called friend and asked could he spare a dime? My friend asked how much did I need? I said, "Whatever you can spare." I'm still waiting on whatever he could spare.

On another occasion, I went to another friend and even offered to do some work for her if possible. I also said to my friend that if she could not help me out, I would understand because times are hard right now for everyone. My friend went so far as to call me to say she had some work for me and she would pay me. I was excited and glad to hear that my friend was willing to help me, so I began working on the project and I attempted to contact my friend on several occasions so that we could go over all of the details of the project. Unfortunately, my friend NEVER got back to me, and basically I am still waiting for her to call me back.

This bothered me because it took a lot for me to even ask for help, and when I did, instead of this person telling me, "No" they couldn't' help me, they lied and said, "Yes". They gave me false hope. And in my eyes, that is the worse thing that you can do to someone, especially someone whom you consider a friend. And what gets me even more, is this person called themselves a Christian.... enough said!

Kimberly C. Kisner

The lesson here is that you can not rely on the promises of man. *(Psalm 146:3 - Do not put your trust in princes, in mortal men, who cannot save.)* You can only rely on the promises of God and yourself…that's it. But it all worked out because in the midst of my turmoil I discovered who my REAL friends were. Now, don't get me wrong I have not put a voodoo curse on those individuals whom I thought were my friends, but I just pray for them and I now know where they stand in my life…they don't!

To Do List

1. Do trust your true friends, they are there to help you.
2. Do not always rely on the promises of others – unfortunately, people will let you down at times.
3. Do know who your REAL friends are.

Kimberly C. Kisner

CHAPTER 13

CAN'T TAKE IT ANYMORE!

BY THIS TIME I STILL HAD NOT found a job. My phone was just not ringing. My e-mail inbox was not overflowing with request for job interviews. My bills just kept piling up. I could not afford to keep my home phone on any longer, nor could I keep the cable on. I was paying my mortgage - minus a couple hundred here and there. I truly felt as though the walls were slowly closing in on me. I couldn't breath. I just didn't know what I was going to do. I was so TIRED of asking my parents and friends for help, I was just so very TIRED.

One day I just broke down and cried for about two hours in the comforts of my home. The tears just kept streaming down my face. I got on my knees and begged and pleaded with God to, "Please help me! I REALLY need a job. I just can't take this anymore!" After my dramatic praying to God, I got up from my knees and wiped the tears from my face, took a hot shower, got dressed and then just went driving to get some fresh air and to clear my thoughts.

I didn't share with my friends or anyone, what took place in the confines of my home. It's not that I was embarrassed…. it was just that I knew that as much as my friends and family loved me, they really couldn't help me with what I was dealing with. I was literally drowning financially, and I was at my wits end. I needed God to hear me, to hear my cry and take care of me.

In case you aren't aware of the awesomeness of God, let me tell you something: He may not come when you need him, but he ALWAYS comes right on time. In that same week of having my "Come to Jesus meeting," one of my best friends from college was having a week long birthday celebration. Yeah, she's known for having some GREAT birthday bashes. Anyway, everyday she planned a different activity for all of her friends to help her celebrate being on earth another year.

So at one of her celebration events, some of my girlfriend's friends from Savannah attended who worked for a university. As we were all sipping on glasses of wine while eating light appetizers, laughing and joking, I said in a half-joking way, "Hey, are you all hiring?" (Addressing one of my friend's guests who came in from Savannah.)

To my surprise, the guest answered, "Yes, we are always hiring!"

Then he asked me to send him my resume.

Hey, he didn't have to ask me twice. As soon as I made it back to my house some time after midnight, I broke out my laptop and immediately e-mailed "my newest friend" my stellar resume. I have to be honest; I really didn't think he would follow through with sharing my resume. So when I ran into him at the next event he said, "Kim, I got your resume and I will pass it on." My mouth said, "Ok, great. Thanks!" but in my mind, I was thinking, "Yeah that's what he says." I guess I was a bit skeptical because I'd been in situations in the past where a potential job connection has said to me, "Forward me your resume and I will pass it on to the right people." Ninety-five percent of the time, they never do what they say they are going to do.

Well, to my surprise, my newest friend made good on what he said he was going to do. It was not even a few days later when the recruiter from the university called and told me that she received my resume and asked if I was interested in the Enrollment Counselor position?

First of all, I was shocked. I couldn't believe that my phone was finally ringing and there was a job opportunity for me. I told the recruiter, "Yes, of course I'm interested." She then went on to tell me what the salary was. The salary was about $60,000 less than what I was used to making, but coming from $320 a week, this was a salary that I could deal with because I would still be able to pay all of my bills and finally, not have to ask for help from my parents or friends.

After we discussed salary, the recruiter informed me that they were doing the first round of interviews that week. I couldn't believe it! Well, I hesitated for a moment because I was a bit under the weather with a touch of the flu, so I didn't feel much up to going to an interview. However, I knew that I had to get a job and I didn't want to miss out on this opportunity. I mean, was this my answer from God? So, I told the recruiter that I would be available to attend the first round of interviews that week.

To Do List

1. Do not be afraid to cry and be vulnerable – it helps to let your frustrations out so they don't build up.
2. Do dust yourself off and get back up and hit the ground running.
3. Do use events, outings, etc., as opportunities to network with others – you never know where your next job will come from.

Kimberly C. Kisner

CHAPTER 14

THE INTERVIEW

THE DAY OF MY INTERVIEW CAME and I knew I needed to pull out all the stops to make a good impression. I put on my sharp, black Calvin Klein pantsuit and my nice black pumps, I had my resume in hand with my nice black briefcase that my mother gave me for Christmas. And of course, my short hair was nicely styled. I was ready for my debut at the university for the Enrollment Counselor position.

I arrived at the university and checked in at the front desk. The receptionist told me where to go. I thought I was going to a waiting area; instead, I was led into a classroom, and to my surprise, I walked into what appeared to be a room full of candidates. I actually thought I was in the wrong room. As it turns out those individuals were also candidates for the Enrollment Counselor position.

I thought this type of interview process was a bit weird because I have NEVER been to a group interview before. Honestly, I thought this was some kind of pyramid scheme where they try to get you to drink the Kool-Aid and you have to pay a certain amount of money to actually get the job.

Well, to my happy surprise, this was not a pyramid scheme. And I didn't have to pay any money to actually get the job. It was an actual group interview where there was a panel of managers and supervisors who asked us questions and we responded.

Additionally, there was an opportunity for us to practice public speaking. We each had to do a five minute speech. Now, I knew about the speech two days in advance, but because I had been sick all week, I didn't feel like writing a speech and I really didn't take the recruiter seriously when she told me that I had to write one. Well, I should have taken her seriously because all of us had to get up and say our speech. And the title of our speech was, "Why should this company hire you?" Indeed and interesting question, but I really didn't feel like answering it.

So as my competition walked up to the podium one-by-one, I realized that they all took it seriously because several of the candidates had note cards and pieces of paper with words that transformed into a speech. So I did what any person would do if they knew that they had to give a speech…that's right, I didn't panic, I just took out a piece of paper and jotted down some bullet points to touch on. I was going to be like a rapper and free style. Ok, I'm not going to bore you with all of the details of my interview process, but I can confidently say that apparently my speech was good enough to get me to the next round of interviews. Thank God.

After my second interview, it only took about one week before I got the call that I was hired, if I was still interested. Ummmm…of course I was. I was overjoyed. However, since I have zero experience with being an Enrollment Counselor, I had to engage in about two weeks of training. Not my favorite thing to do, but at least I was employed again. The only stipulation was that I was hired on a three month contract, which means that after 90 days, if my performance met the university's expectations, then I would be asked to come aboard in a more permanent capacity.

Kimberly C. Kisner

Again, I didn't have a problem with that because I was going to be the best Enrollment Counselor that I could be. And even though the pay was substantially less than what I was used too, again, it was better than $320 a week.

Are you familiar with the phrase; "You find a job when you have one?"

Well, even though I'm grateful for this job and I truly believe that I'm where I am supposed to be at this point in my life, I still find myself on the various job sites looking for a position in my field that is more along the lines of what I'm used to as it relates to compensation.

You see, you have to learn how to "Rest in the will of God." You have to understand that God may not come when you want him to, but he does come on time. And he may not give you exactly what you "think" you deserve, but he gives you what you need. In my case, I felt like God had forgotten about me sometimes because I was waiting for a job for eight months. In my mind, that felt like a lifetime. However, I've spoken to individuals who have been waiting for a year or more for a job and some are still waiting.

In case you were wondering, "No, in my mind God didn't come through when I wanted him to…but he did come just in time." It's funny because one week after I started the job as an Enrollment Counselor, I received a notice in the mail stating that my unemployment funds had run out, and I was eligible to apply for an extension to receive about six more months of unemployment. When I received that letter and read it, all I could do is laugh and say, "Thank you God. You were right on time."

I say all this to say that your first job after being unemployed for however long, may not be your "dream job" but it may be a job that will allow you to gain additional skill sets that you've never had or allow you

Kimberly C. Kisner

to utilize a different part of the brain that you normally don't get to use. Additionally, it could be just a "mean time" job that will help you catch up on some back bills and get you back on solid financial footing again. More importantly, this may be the job that leads to your dream job.

Remember what I just said, "You get a job when you have a job."

It is important that you learn how to rest in the will of God and to be thankful that he came through when you needed him. Be happy and joyful about the job he's blessed you with. Sometimes God blesses us with things that we don't appreciate. With so little faith, you may miss the other blessings that he has in store for you.

It's like God blessing me with a 3 bedroom, 2 1/2 bath townhouse (my starter home) that I've been in for about six years. Now, let's say I want a larger house with a deck (which I actually do want) and I don't take care of my townhouse, as far as keeping it clean etc. Do you actually think that God is going to bless me with a bigger house with a deck, just because I want it? I would venture to say, no, at least not until I learn to take care of and appreciate what I have in my townhouse.

The same principle applies as it relates to a new job or an old job for that matter. Every morning I wake up now and thank God for this new opportunity and I have a smile on my face and a positive attitude because I don't know what else God may have in store for me as it relates to my career and other aspects of my life.

You see, this layoff experience has taught me a lot about myself and life. Yes, being laid off more times than I could ever imagine was a very uncomfortable experience. However, those experiences have taught me to be perseverant, persistent, patient and full of possibilities.

I also realized that sometimes our "egos" get in the way of our progress. We allow the "ego" to think that we are immune to certain things, as though we are above being affected by "bad" situations. When those thoughts occur in our heads and we walk around thinking, "It can't happen to me!" It is at that moment that we can become humbled by God.

I'm sorry if I'm getting too religious, but being striped down to your low point can really humble you. I know that my last layoff with the church really humbled me, and now my outlook and perspective on life is different. I learned some very valuable lessons.

For example, it's not enough to just rely on that job where you work for someone else. It is important to have a plan "B," and that plan "B" should be considering self-employment - whether it be part time or full time – because it is important to always strive to be self-sufficient. You see, by being self-employed you don't have to worry about HR handing you your walking papers. You only have yourself to blame if you don't make any money.

There's much more information and tips you may find helpful so keep on reading.

To Do List

1. Do look at your next job as an opportunity.
2. Do learn to rest in "His" will.
3. Do have a plan B.
4. Do be persistent, patient and full of possibilities.

Kimberly C. Kisner

CHAPTER 15

HEALTHCARE AND THE ART OF NEGOTIATION

TIP 14
MAKE NO MISTAKE, YOU DO NEED HEALTHCARE INSURANCE.

USUALLY WHEN YOU GET LAID OFF from a company, you have the option of maintaining your healthcare benefits through COBRA. However, paying into COBRA can be expensive. At times, COBRA can cost as much as a car note, that's why you must consider other healthcare options.

Now I know that you are probably wondering, "How in the world can I afford healthcare when I don't have a job?" But take it from me; it's worth it to have minimum coverage because you never know when you will need to see a doctor. There's nothing worse than going to the doctor or having some kind of medical emergency, and then having to pay out of your pocket - or worse, a doctor may not see you without insurance.

I opted not to utilize the expensive COBRA benefits, and purchased

Kimberly C. Kisner

healthcare from Humana One. It was a little more that $100 a month, but it was worth it. However, I have had much better healthcare coverage at my previous places of employment. But in the meantime, COBRA works. If you need a list of affordable health care options, just get on Google or go to www.Coverageforall.com.

TIP 15
KILL YOUR BILL COLLECTORS WITH KINDNESS.

I'm almost positive that you've heard the adage, "Kill them with kindness," right? Well, I've always secretly thought that I would be a great lawyer, and now after dealing with bill collectors during my layoff period, I'm certain that I would have been awesome in the courtroom.

During your layoff period it is important that you try your best to pay your bills. Now, you may not be able to pay them on time, but you need to at least make a real effort – and most important, communication is critical. I found that when you contact your bill collector i.e. utility company, mortgage company, car loan company, etc...you need to be straightforward and honest. Luckily for me, the economy was in a recession, so practically everyone was making payment arrangements or extensions.

When contacting your bill collector there are a few tips that you will need to keep in mind:

1. *Call them with a smile on your face* - I know that this sounds crazy, but people can hear and feel when you are smiling on the phone. And when you are smiling you give off a pleasant and friendly vibe which in turn makes the person on the other end feel good.

2. *Be honest or "keep it real"* – Just be honest. Don't try to pull the wool over their eyes. Seriously, they have heard every excuse in

the book. You are not trying to get a day off from work; you are trying to negotiate the terms of the money that you owe. By being honest you show that you have integrity and character and that you are not trying to take advantage of the situation.

Let's face it, you do owe the money and just because you aren't working, doesn't mean that the bills will stop. In my case, I always told the truth about my situation. I informed them that I was laid off and I also told them how much money I receive every week from unemployment, then I explain that I'm simply trying to stay afloat by trying to keep my house, my car and my utilities paid, and if I have enough after that, food on the table.

3. *Make good on your payment arrangements* - This is imperative. If you make a promise to pay arrangements, please... please....please...keep your promise. You can avoid missing your payment arrangement deadlines by making realistic payment arrangements that you know you will be able to meet. To be sure that you don't forget the agreement, write it down on a calendar and put it in your Blackberry, PDA, cell phone, or outlook calendar. Whatever you use to remember appointments, that's what you use to keep track of your payment arrangements.

Now, I do understand that life happens and sometimes your money gets very funny. That's ok because all you have to do is contact that bill collector prior to your scheduled payment arrangement, and let them know what's going on. Usually, they will work with you and offer you another arrangement, but you CAN'T miss the second payment arrangement date.

4. *Try Not to Stress* - If you don't have it to give then you just don't have it. There have been plenty of times when my cable

service or my home phone line had to be cut off completely. I remember telling the cable company, "Hey, I don't know what to tell you, I just don't have it. So if you must turn it off, so be it." Because honestly, do I really need HBO? and quite frankly, do I really need a home phone line? Ummm...no, not really to both.

Don't get me wrong, I'm a TV lover, and most important, I LOVE, LOVE watching movies. But when it comes to budgeting, I really don't need all of those premium stations any way.

As for my home phone line, well no one calls me on it except for my parents and the bill collectors. Most people call me on my cell phone. The only reason I need a phone line is for my high speed Internet. (Which incidentally, I no longer have either).

These are things that you think about during your layoff period. Understand this: some of the things in our lives that we think are necessities really aren't. And while we may enjoy watching cable or having call waiting and caller ID, they are really just "nice to haves" - you don't need them. Unfortunately, in order to enjoy TV, you need at least basic cable. Short of that you can go to Blockbuster or go to the movies or join NetFlix. For less than the price of admission of going to the movies with a buddy ($16.99/month), you can watch as many movies and TV show series as you'd like to from the comfort of your own home – at least until you get your finances back on track.

To Do List

1. Do get health insurance.
2. Do be honest and polite with your bill collectors – it does pay off.
3. Do take stock of what is a necessity in your life.

Kimberly C. Kisner

CHAPTER 16

GET OUT OF YOUR OWN WAY – MAKE IT HAPPEN!

TIP 16
FURTHER YOUR EDUCATION.

OK HAVE YOU EVER WANTED to further your education, but either you didn't have the money or other things in life just happened? Your layoff period is an excellent time to go back and get that degree, whether it be your Associates, Bachelors, Masters, Law Degree or PhD, this is the perfect time. Seriously, you have nothing but time on your hands. While you are sitting on the couch watching Oprah, you could be getting your life together as it relates to education and strive to be the "Oprah" in your own world.

Take it from me, I was unemployed for about eight months, if I didn't already have two degrees, I would have most certainly used the time that I was out of work to at least start working towards another degree. The great thing about school is, for many people they don't have to worry about paying for it until about six months after graduation (If they utilize financial aid). If you are a person who doesn't test well and you don't want to take the GRE or the GMAT, there are several universities out there that don't require either of those.

Perhaps you are someone who is considering going to law school? Well during your down time you could study for the LSAT. Honestly, you wouldn't have any other distractions in your life besides looking for a job, and quite frankly, looking for a job can be boring at times. You can only devote so many hours a day looking for a job. You can apply the rest of your time studying for the LSAT.

My point is, ladies and gentlemen, you should use your down time wisely and go back to school if it's something that you've been putting off.

TIP 17
LEARN TO BE CREATIVE.

It's time to think outside of YOUR box! Being out of work for eight months was very interesting for me because all I've ever known, since I started my career, are the fields of communications and marketing. So, I really didn't think that I could do anything else, or maybe I wasn't even open to the possibilities of dreaming of doing anything else. I LOVED being in the field of communications/marketing. I didn't want to do anything else.

However, what I found was that jobs in the field of marketing/communications are few and far between. They just weren't out there. The few that I applied for, I received no responses. As I mentioned early in this book, I applied everywhere - from Walmart to Walgreens to Pearl Vision - and then of course, I ended up landing a job with the a certain university as an Enrollment Counselor.

One of the responsibilities of an Enrollment Counselor is to be on the phone most of your eight hour-day. I remember the Director of Enrollment asking me in my interview, what was going to be the most challenging aspect of the Enrollment Counselor position? I had to be honest (and I knew that my answer could prevent me from getting this job, but I had to say it). My answer was, "Talking on the phone for most of the day." However, I did follow it up with, "but I'm not afraid of a challenge."

You see, when the economy is bad and the unemployment rate is high, you have to accept the position that there are few choices. You have to step outside of your comfort zone and determine the other type of skills you posses that can help you to obtain a job. Once you open your mind, you will start looking at the various jobs that are available to you with a different perspective. Trust me! I know.

To Do List

1. Do be resourceful and think "outside the box".
2. Do think about furthering your education – it's never too late to learn.
3. Do think about "all" of the skills that you have to offer.

Kimberly C. Kisner

CHAPTER 17

MONEY ISN'T EVERYTHING

TIP 18
There will Never be Enough Money!

I'M JUST GOING TO BE HONEST WITH YOU, the job that I landed as an Enrollment Counselor was paying me about $60,000 less than I made prior to be being laid off twice in 2008 when I was a Communications Manager and a Marketing Director. I haven't made $34,000 since I graduated from college. The reality for me was that I had a house, car and other responsibilities, so making $34,000 when I was living at home in Cleveland with my mom and didn't have a mortgage to pay was okay. Additionally, when I purchased my house, I was making about $52,000, so how in the world would I be able to afford my house, my car etc… with a salary of $34,000?

Well, I tell you, things happen in life for a reason and sometimes you don't know what that reason is until something else in your life happens and then a light goes off in your head. You have what Oprah calls an "Ah-ha moment!" Lucky for me about a year and a half ago, I decided to

Kimberly C. Kisner

re-finance my house into a fixed rate (this was before the recession and bad economy hit). I refinanced because I had an adjustable rate mortgage and every year it would go up a little. Because of refinancing, I now have a mortgage that is affordable. In fact, it's low enough where I can handle it with a salary of $34,000. Ok so now, as I look back at that time when I re-financed, I am really grateful that I did.

My other "Ah-ha moment" was when I realized that "I was able to make it just fine on $320 a week of unemployment, and the occasional help from family and friends." Now, granted I couldn't always afford the luxury activities such as shopping, manicures and pedicures (every two weeks), etc., but I was still able to pay my bills and enjoy life. I think I was even able to go out of town a few times.

You see, the reality is, you're always going to think you need more money. If you are making $50,000, you think you need $60,000. If you're making $70,000, you think you need $80,000. The bottom line is, it's all about budgeting and learning what you really need. I am so blessed to have made great salaries for most of my career. So I've been able to buy what I want, splurge and delve into some of the finer things in life. Now, I'm just scaling back and really appreciating the art of budgeting.

Sure, I would like to get back to my usual salary, but until that day comes, I have to be thankful and work with what I have because, right now, there are still folks out there who don't have jobs and don't know when their next job is coming. So thank you Lord for hearing my prayer and answering it. My time will come again, just like your time will come for getting another job. TRUST GOD!!! Like the good ole saying goes, God may not answer your prayers when you want him to, but he always answers them right on time! And I am a true testament of that fact.

Kimberly C. Kisner

TIP 19
NEW CAREER GOALS.

Remember when I told you that sometimes the first job you secure after being unemployed may just be a job to get you by until the job you really want comes along? This was definitely the case for me. The job at the university is not a job, that under normal circumstances, I would even think about applying for however, it was the only company that was ringing my phone to hire me at the time.

With the university, I had to look at this as a new adventure and a new opportunity. I had to decide what my destiny was going to be with this company, as long as I was employed there. I had to make decisions about my career. Now mind you, I still found myself looking for other jobs that were more in my "deserved" salary range and within the areas of my expertise. However, until the day comes for me to move on from the university, I have to decide what my future might look like while employed there.

In my research, I considered various jobs that met my career requirements and those particular jobs are the ones I'm striving to obtain while working at the university. You see, I don't have any idea what God has in store for me, but I do know that right now he wants me working at the university. True, the money is not the best, but this too shall pass and eventually I will find myself making the type of salary that I'm accustomed to.

So you're probably wondering, "Ok Kim, what is your point?"

My point is, while you have a job, you must figure out how to leverage that position into another one in the company that pays a higher salary. Even if you are on fries at the local fast food establishment, you need to focus on what you need to do to master the art of working the fries

Kimberly C. Kisner

and what other positions you can strive for. Those positions may include, shift manager, cashier manager or even store manager. No matter what it is, you have to stay motivated and strive toward your ultimate career goal, even if it's not in the "career" that you want right now.

I will tell you this much, while working at the university, I have gained valuable skill sets that I didn't know I had or that I needed. Another important thing is, while on your new job, you must be focused, committed and have a positive attitude. The reason being is because you never know who's watching you. Believe me, you are being watched! Whether it's a fellow co-worker, a manager/supervisor, or even a customer, you are being watched! You never know what kind of opportunities may come your way by being committed, focused and having a positive attitude. Oh, I almost forgot having a good work ethic also is key. You'd be surprised at how far a good work ethic goes.

Well, I'm just about all out of tips and advice for you. I really do hope that my layoff experiences have given you encouragement and guidance as you go through this period in your life. Folks, I know it's rough and financially challenging, but I promise you can over come this.

The key is to remember that you are not ALONE. This isn't just happening to you. There are other people in the same position as you or even worse. One of the things that I always tell myself is, "It could be worse." and it definitely could be worse. I was fortunate that I didn't have any children, because if I did, my circumstances may have been a lot tougher. But since it is just me, I only have to worry about providing for myself. Since it was just me, I could get away with having cereal everyday or eating once or twice a day instead of three times to save money.

Sure I had to seriously budget and I couldn't always do the things I was accustomed to, but my phone isn't ringing and I'm able to pay my bills without having to negotiate. To me, that's what matters. I still have

Kimberly C. Kisner

my house and my car. I know there are plenty of individuals who can't say that. So while I'm not working at my dream job, making my dream salary....I am making enough to survive and that's saying a lot, considering that I wasn't sure if I was going to make it.

To Do List

1. Do make do with what you have – you will be surprised that you really can make it.
2. Do prioritize the various things that you like to do – you can still do them just not as often.
3. Do look at that new job as a new adventure-it may not be what you want but it may be what you need at that moment.
4. Do have good work ethic – it will take you a long way.

Kimberly C. Kisner

CHAPTER 18

THE LAYOFF TOOL KIT

HAVING A REDUCED INCOME is definitely unfortunate. But there are things that you can do to ease some of your financial burdens. Just because you are faced with a reduction in income doesn't mean you can't take control of how to handle the situation.

One of the most difficult aspects (for me) of having a reduce income is accepting the realization that I couldn't spend as much as I was accustomed to. I couldn't shop the way I normally do or get those manicures and pedicures as frequently or just hop on a plane to get out of town for the weekend when I wanted to.

With a reduction in income, you can't be in a state of denial and pretend that nothing in your pocket book or wallet has changed. Being in denial unfortunately won't change the fact that you are in a financial cul-de-sac. You have to be financially mature enough to realize that you need to find various ways to reduce your spending and increase your income. It is important for you to know where you are financially so you can adjust your spending. The following steps will help you to deal with your reduced income:

Step #1: Figure out how much money you have coming into your household –Write down the amount of money you had coming in on a monthly basis prior to the layoff. Then write down the amount of monthly income you currently have to spend. You will need to know how much income you have to work with. Make sure you include all of the income from everyone in your household (if you live alone – then just focus on your income). Include paychecks (or severance payments), unemployment compensation, child support, alimony, or government assistance.

Step#2: Refer to your past spending habits to estimate your expenses prior to the layoff. (You can figure this out by looking at your checkbook or expense receipts), then write down your monthly expenses. Now identify areas where you can reduce your spending.

It may be hard for the ladies to give up those bi-weekly manicures and pedicures or for the fellas to give up those must have gadgets. If you even cut out some of the smallest expenses, you may be surprised at how much money you could save.

For example, prior to being laid off, I bet you went out to lunch almost every day. Going out to lunch probably costs you about $6.00 - $10.00 a day, which amounts to about $30.00 - $50.00 a week which equates to about $120.00 - $200.00 a month. If you eliminate going out to lunch every day and bring your lunch, you would save yourself about $120.00 - $200.00 per month. Those monies can be used to pay some of your bills.

What about cutting out coupons? I know that means you have to purchase a Sunday paper. I'm sure you can come up with $2.00 for a paper filled with double coupons. Those coupons will help reduce your grocery bill by almost half. One thing that I did to help save money on groceries was to obtain a Kroger Plus Card. Although, I like shopping at Publix better, when I need to save some money on groceries I go to

Kimberly C. Kisner

Kroger's and use my magical savings card.

Step#3 Renegotiate the terms of your mortgage and car note. I mentioned the art of negotiating your bills earlier in the book. But this step is very crucial for those of you who have houses and cars. If you are like me, you don't want to lose your house nor your car. The key thing to remember is you can't be afraid to contact your mortgage or car lender.

Regarding your mortgage, a loan can be restructured to give you a reduced or modified interest rate which in turn gives you a lower payment. Given the current economic conditions, there are plenty of loan modification programs available to you that will assist you with making your mortgage payments.

As it relates to your car loan, you can call your lender and ask for an extension or a deferment. However, in order to get assistance, you have to ask for help, otherwise, you could be setting yourself up to lose your house and car. Your lenders don't know what's going on in your life unless you tell them. Save yourself the stress and heartache and give them a call as soon as you find out that you are laid off with impending financial difficulty.

As you complete your income and expense chart, here are some important expenses to keep in mind on a monthly basis:

Books, newspapers	Food	Prescriptions
Cable	Gas for car	School Supplies
Car payment	Housing	Shoe repair
Clothing	Internet	Tithes
Credit cards	Membership dues	Tuition/fees
Education	Personal Care	Utilities
Entertainment	Phone/Cell phone	

Again, you can't be afraid to face your debts, because unfortunately they do not go away when your income decreases. Taking inventory of all of your expenses will help you in conversations with creditors, when asking for help to establish a modified repayment plan that will reduce your payments to a more manageable level. However, I can't stress enough that you need to communicate with creditors ASAP, so that they can determine how to help you with your bills, before paying them becomes a problem.

I hope that my tips and advice have helped to ease your mind about layoffs, if not, think about this: you have to shift your perception about your situation. You have to have positive thoughts, because positive thoughts attract things in your life that make you feel good about yourself and the state of your life. Being positive will help you to get through your jobless situation.

Think about the things in your life that you are grateful for.

One of the thoughts that keeps me going is thinking about my experiences with some of the finer things in life, such as hopping on a plane whenever I wanted to leave, spa appointments or shopping. If I never get to experience that type of lifestyle again and making $90,000 a year again, I can honestly say that I wouldn't be upset. At least I had the opportunity to experience that type of economic freedom.

You see, it's not all about money and the material things, it's about your spirit, your character - it's about being a survivor! It's about you resting in the will of God and making it through the storm. You can do it...you can make it through the storm...you may be laid off, but you are never laid out! Remember that.

Kimberly C. Kisner

ADDITIONAL RESOURCES

- www.careerbuilder.com
- www.monster.com
- www.randstad.com
- www.vault.com
- www.careeronestop.org

Kimberly C. Kisner